Israel's Biblical Right to the Land

"I will give your descendants all the land I promised them and it will be their inheritance forever."

Exodus 32:13

Compiled by Rev. Kaatee Bailey

Other Books by Rev. Kaatee Bailey
God's Judgment on the Nations

Other Books Soon Available:
Israel's Historical Rights to the Land

Israel's Legal Rights to the Land

Israel's Archaeological Rights to the Land

This book compiled by Rev. Kaatee Bailey is provided as a reference guide regarding the land of Israel. It is comprised of accumulated Scriptures from the Old Testament (Tanakh) which positively validates the Jewish claim to the land of Israel. The Scripture quotations used are from various easy to read translations of the Holy Bible. The books of the Bible used are written in English and Hebrew.

Compiled by Rev. Kaatee Bailey

Copyright 2013 First Edition
Published by The Hawaii-Israel Alignment
ISBN 0615914144

Forward

This book illuminates an understanding of God's divine plan for mankind and His undisputable covenant promise to the land of Israel and the Jewish People.

Thank you Kaatee, for I have been truly blessed by your inspirational, steadfast dedication and your heartfelt love for Israel. May Yeshua's blessing follow you wherever His hand may lead you.

Your Dear Friend

Nowlin Correa

Founder of KeHilat HaMishkan

Co-coordinator of 'The Hawaii Israel Alignment'

Israel's Biblical Right to the Land

Introduction

This book is comprised of accumulated Scriptures that establish God's land grant to Abraham, Isaac, Jacob and their descendants. The Holy Scripture, God highest written authority clearly defines the original and rightful owners of the land of Israel. His Word that stands unchanged and eternally true states that God Himself gave the land of Israel to the Jewish people. Israel is the only nation of the world whose land deed was signed by God, Himself. In the Old Testament Scripture (Tanakh), which is held sacred to both Jew and Christian, are recorded Israel's history and her people's oldest recorded deeds and land grants reserved for them.

Even though Israel rebelled against God and was exiled from the land, God's land covenant and unconditional promise to them was never annulled to his Chosen People, nor did it abrogate their right to the land of Israel. God's sworn oath was an everlasting possession to the Jewish people and their exile from Israel was only temporary. God assures the Jewish people of their perpetual right to the land of Israel by reiterating His oath more than forty times in Scriptures.

God's dealings with the children of Israel involve His faithfulness more than their faithfulness. We should recognize that God's promises concerning the Jewish people are based on the one who made them and not on whether or not the recipients of the promises deserve them. No one deserves the mercy and grace of God, but He extends them to all of us anyway. *He will keep his covenant forever, his promises for a thousand generations. (Psalm 105:8).* Let there be no doubt that the land of Israel belongs to the Jews, and God intends to keep all the promises He made to the Jewish people. *The Lord appeared to Abram and said, "To your descendants I will give this Land" (Genesis 12:7) ... "And I will give to you and to your descendants after you, the land where you now reside as a foreigner and, all the land of Canaan, for an everlasting possession" (Genesis 17:8).*

The nations surrounding Israel would like to claim the land of Israel for their personal possession. Even though, a majority of the Jewish people were exiled from the land, that doesn't give anyone else the right to claim the land of Israel for their own. The Jewish people have had a deep connection with the land of Israel for more than 3,000 years, and a continuous physical presence there.

If a landlord has some bad tenants that he evicts from his property, he does not expect anyone else to enter his vacant property and claim it for their own. The Landlord of Israel evicted most of the Jewish people from the land, but that didn't give the Romans, the Byzantines, the Crusaders, the Ottomans or the Arabs the right to claim God's holy land for themselves. Those who challenge the legitimacy of modern Israel belonging to the Jews, disregard Jewish history, ideals and values.

According to God's title deed, the land of Israel for the Jewish People is an everlasting possession, which means endless,

4

never-ending and forever. God's Word, the supreme and utmost authority establishes the Jewish People as the rightful and legal owners of all the land of Israel.

God's Land Covenant to Israel is *"Forever"*

The following verses describe God's unyielding commitment to Israel and His assurance to the Jewish people of the perpetual right to the Land of Israel as an everlasting possession.

Leviticus 26:44-45

"Yet in spite of this (Israel's disobedience), when they are in the land of their enemies, I will not reject them, nor will I so abhor them as to destroy them, breaking My covenant with them; for I am the Lord their God. But **I will remember for them the covenant with their ancestors**."

Psalms 105:8-11

He has remembered His covenant forever, the word which He commanded **to a thousand generations**, and the covenant which He made with Abraham, and His oath to Isaac. Then **He confirmed it to Jacob for a statute, to Israel as an everlasting covenant**, saying, **"To you I will give the land of Canaan as the portion of your inheritance."**

Genesis 17:7

The Lord appeared to Abram and said, **"To your descendants I will give this Land."** God further said to Abraham; **"I will establish my covenant between me and you and your descendants after you throughout their generations for an everlasting covenant**, to be God to you and to your descendants after you."

Genesis 17:5-8

No longer will you be called Abram; your name will be Abraham, for I have made you a father of many nations. I will make you very fruitful; I will make nations of you, and kings will come from you. I will establish my covenant as an everlasting covenant between me and you and your descendants after you for the generations to come, to be your God and the God of your descendants after you. **The whole land of Canaan, where you now reside as a foreigner, I will give as an everlasting possession to you and your descendants after you;** and I will be their God."

Genesis 13:14-15

After Lot left, the Lord said to Abram, "Look around you. Look north, south, east, and west. **All this land that you see I will give to you and your offspring forever."**

Genesis 17:18-19

Abraham said to God, "Oh that Ishmael might live before you."

But God said, "No, but Sarah your wife shall bear you a son, and you shall call his name Isaac; **and I will establish my covenant with him for an everlasting covenant for his descendants after him.**"

1 Chronicles 16:15-18

He remembers his covenant forever, the promise he made, for a thousand generations, the covenant he made with Abraham, the oath he swore to Isaac. He confirmed it to Jacob as a decree, O Israel as an everlasting covenant: "**To you I will give the land of Canaan as the portion you will inherit.**"

Judges 2:1

"**I will never break my covenant with you.**"

Isaiah 60:21

"Then all your people will be righteous and **they will possess the land forever.** They are the shoot I have planted, the work of my hands, for the display of my splendor."

8

Scriptural Promises Establishing

Israel's Biblical Right to the Land

Genesis – Bereshit

Genesis 12:5-7
Abram took his wife Sarai, his nephew Lot, all the possessions they had accumulated and the people they had acquired in Harran, and they set out for the land of Canaan, and they arrived there. Abram traveled through the land as far as the site of the great tree of Moreh at Shechem. At that time the Canaanites were in the land. **The Lord appeared to Abram and said, "To your offspring I will give this land."** So he built an altar there to the Lord, who had appeared to him.

Genesis 13: 14-17
After Lot left, the Lord said to Abram, "Look around from where you are, to the north and south, to the east and west. **All the land that you see I will give to you and your offspring forever.** I will make your offspring like the dust of the earth, so that if anyone could count the dust, then your offspring could be counted. **Go walk through the length and breadth of the land, for I am giving it to you."**

Genesis 15:5-7
He took him outside and said, "Look up at the sky and count the stars if indeed you can count them." Then he said to him, "So

shall your offspring be." Abram believed the Lord, and he credited it to him as righteousness. He also said, "**I am the Lord, who brought you out of Ur of the Chaldeans to give you this land to take possession of it.**"

Genesis 15:18-21
On that day the Lord made a covenant with Abram and said, "**to your descendants I give this land, from the Wadi of Egypt to the great river, the Euphrates**—the land of the Kenites, Kenizzites, Kadmonites, Hittites, Perizzites, Rephaites, Amorites, Canaanites, Girgashites and Jebusites."

Genesis 17: 7-8
"**I will establish my covenant as an everlasting covenant between me and you and your descendants after you for the generations to come**, to be your God and the God of your descendants after you. **The whole land of Canaan, where you now reside as a foreigner, I will give as an everlasting possession to you and your descendants after you;** and I will be their God."

Genesis 25:5-6
Abraham left everything he owned to Isaac. But while he was still living, he gave gifts to the sons of his concubines and sent them away from his son Isaac to the land of the east.

Genesis 26:2-4

The Lord appeared to Isaac and said, "Do not go down to Egypt; stay in the land of which I shall tell you. Sojourn in this land and I will be with you and bless you, for to you and to your descendants **I will give all these lands, and I will establish the oath which I swore to your father Abraham. I will** multiply your descendants as the stars of heaven, and will **give your descendants all these lands;** and by you descendants all the nations of the earth shall be blessed."

Genesis 28:4

May he give you and your descendants the blessing given to Abraham, **so that you may take possession of the land where you now reside as a foreigner, the land God gave to Abraham.**

Genesis 28:10-13

Jacob left Beersheba and set out for Harran. When he reached a certain place, he stopped for the night because the sun had set. Taking one of the stones there, he put it under his head and lay down to sleep. He had a dream in which he saw a stairway resting on the earth, with its top reaching to heaven, and the angels of God were ascending and descending on it. There above it stood the Lord, and he said: **"I am the Lord, the God of your father Abraham and the God of Isaac. I will give you and your descendants the land on which you are lying."**

Genesis 35:12

"<u>The Land which I gave to Abraham and Isaac, I will give it to</u> <u>you, and I will give the Land to your descendants after you.</u>"

Genesis 48:3-4

Jacob said to Joseph, "God Almighty appeared to me at Luz in the land of Canaan, and there he blessed me and said to me, "I am going to make you fruitful and increase your numbers. <u>I</u> <u>will make you a community of peoples, and I will give this land</u> <u>as an everlasting possession to your descendants after you.</u>"

Genesis 50:24

Then Joseph said to his brothers, "I am about to die. But **God will** surely come to your aid and **take you up out of this land to the** **land he promised on oath to Abraham, Isaac and Jacob.**

Exodus – Shemot

Exodus 3:8
So **I have come down** to rescue them from the hand of the Egyptians and **to bring them up out of that land into a good and spacious land, a land flowing with milk and honey**; the home of the Canaanites, Hittites, Amorites, Perizzites, Hivites and Jebusites.

Exodus 3:17
And **I have promised to bring you up** out of your misery in Egypt **into the land of the Canaanites, Hittites, Amorites, Perizzites, Hivites and Jebusites to a land flowing with milk and honey**.

Exodus 6:2-4
God also said to Moses, "I am the Lord. I appeared to Abraham, to Isaac and to Jacob as God Almighty, but by my name the Lord I did not make myself fully known to them. **I also established my covenant with them to give them the land of Canaan, where they resided as foreigners.**"

Exodus 6:8

"I made a great promise to Abraham, Isaac, and Jacob. <u>I promised to give them a special land. So I will lead you to that land. I will give you that land. It will be yours. I am the Lord.</u>"

Exodus 12:25

<u>When you enter the land that the Lord will give you as he promised</u>, and observe this ceremony (Passover)...

Exodus 13:3-5

Then Moses said to the people, "Commemorate this day, the day you came out of Egypt, out of the land of slavery, because the Lord brought you out of it with a mighty hand. Eat nothing containing yeast. Today, in the month of Aviv, you are leaving. <u>When the Lord brings you into the land of the Canaanites, Hittites, Amorites, Hivites and Jebusites, the land he swore to your ancestors to give you, a land flowing with milk and honey</u>, you are to observe this ceremony in this month."

Exodus 13:11

<u>After the Lord brings you into the land of the Canaanites and gives it to you, as he promised on oath to you and your ancestors.</u>

Exodus 20:12

Honor your father and your mother, so **that you may live long in the land the Lord your God is giving you.**

Exodus 23:23

My angel will go ahead of you and **bring you into the land of the Amorites, Hittites, Perizzites, Canaanites, Hivites and Jebusites,** and I will wipe them out.

Exodus 23:31

"I will establish your borders from the Red Sea to the Mediterranean Sea, and from the desert to the Euphrates River. I will give into your hands the people who live in the land, and you will drive them out before you."

Exodus 32:11-13

But Moses begged the Lord his God, "Lord, don't let your anger destroy your people. You brought them out of Egypt with your great power and strength. But if you destroy your people, the Egyptians will say, 'God planned to do bad things to his people. That is why he led them out of Egypt. He wanted to kill them in the mountains. He wanted to wipe them off the earth.' So don't be angry with your people. Please change your mind! Don't destroy them. **Remember Abraham, Isaac, and Israel.** These men served you, and you used your name to make a promise to them. You said, "**I will give your people all this land as I promised. This land will be theirs forever.**"

Exodus 33:1-3

Then the Lord said to Moses, "Leave this place, you and the people you brought up out of Egypt, **and go up to the land I promised on oath to Abraham, Isaac and Jacob," saying, "I will give it to your descendants."**

Leviticus – Vayikrah

Leviticus 14:34-35
"**When you enter the land of Canaan, which I am giving you as your possession,** and I put a spreading mold in a house in that land, the owner of the house must go and tell the priest, 'I have seen something that looks like a defiling mold in my house.'

Leviticus 20:24
But I said to you, "**You will possess their land; I will give it to you as an inheritance, a land flowing with milk and honey.** I am the Lord your God, who has set you apart from the nations."

Leviticus 25:2
Speak to the Israelites and say to them; "**When you enter the land I am going to give you**, the land itself must observe a Sabbath to the Lord."

Leviticus 25:23
"**The land must not be sold** permanently, because **the land is mine and you reside in my land as foreigners and strangers.**"

Leviticus 25:38

I am the Lord your God, who brought you out of Egypt to give you the land of Canaan and to be your God.

Leviticus 26:42

I will remember my covenant with Jacob and my covenant with Isaac and my covenant with Abraham, **and I will remember the land**.

Leviticus 26:44-45

Yet in spite of this, **when they are in the land of their enemies, I will not reject them or abhor them so as to destroy them completely, breaking my covenant with them.** I am the Lord their God. But **for their sake I will remember the covenant with their ancestors** whom I brought out of Egypt in the sight of the nations to be their God. I am the Lord.

Numbers – Bamidbar

Numbers 10:29
Moses said to Hobab, "<u>We are traveling to the land that the Lord promised to give to us.</u> Come with us and we will be good to you. The Lord has promised good things to the Israelites."

Numbers 11:12
Did I conceive all these people? Did I give them birth? Why do you tell me to carry them in my arms, as a nurse carries an infant, <u>**to the land you promised on oath to their ancestors?**</u>

Numbers 13:2
"Send some men to explore **the land of Canaan, which I am giving to the Israelites.** From each ancestral tribe send one of its leaders."

Numbers 15:2
"Speak to the Israelites and say to them: '**<u>After you enter the land I am giving you as a home</u>** and you present to the Lord food offerings from the herd or the flock, as an aroma pleasing to the Lord—whether burnt offerings or sacrifices, for special vows or freewill offerings or festival offerings— then the person who brings an offering shall present to the Lord a grain offering

of a tenth of an ephah of the finest flour mixed with a quarter of a hin of olive oil.'

Numbers 26:55
"**Be sure that the land is distributed by lot**. What each group inherits will be according to the names for its ancestral tribe."

Numbers 27:12
Then the Lord said to Moses, "**Go up this mountain in the Abarim Range and see the land I have given the Israelites.**"

Numbers 32:20-22
Then Moses said to them, "If you will do this—if you will arm yourselves before the Lord for battle and if all of you who are armed cross over the Jordan before the Lord until he has driven his enemies out before him— then when the land is subdued before the Lord, you may return and be free from your obligation to the Lord and to Israel. **And this land will be your possession before the Lord.**"

Numbers 33:53-54
Take possession of the land and settle in it, for I have given you the land to possess. Distribute the land by lot, according to your clans. To a larger group give a larger inheritance, and to a smaller group a smaller one. Whatever falls to them by lot will be theirs. Distribute it according to your ancestral tribes.

Numbers 34:2

Speak to the Israelites and tell them this; **"You will soon enter The land of Canaan. I am giving you that land to be your very own."**

Numbers 34:12-13

Then the boundary will go down along the Jordan and end at the Dead Sea. **"This will be your land,** with its boundaries on every side." Moses commanded the Israelites, **"Assign this land by lot as an inheritance.** The Lord has ordered that it be given to the nine and a half tribes."

Numbers 34:29

These are the men the Lord commanded to **assign the inheritance to the Israelites in the land of Canaan.**

Deuteronomy – Devarim

Deuteronomy 1:8
"See, **I have given you this land. Go in and take possession of the land** the Lord swore he would give to your fathers, to Abraham, Isaac and Jacob and to their descendants after them."

Deuteronomy 1:21
"See, **the Lord your God has given you the land. Go up and take possession of it as the Lord, the God of your ancestors, told you.** Do not be afraid; do not be discouraged."

Deuteronomy 1:25
Taking with them some of the fruit of the land, they brought it down to us and reported, **"It is a good land that the Lord our God is giving us."**

Deuteronomy 1:38-39
But your helper, Joshua son of Nun, will go into the land. Encourage Joshua, because **he will lead the Israelites to take the land for their own.** You thought your little children would be taken by your enemies. **But those children, who are still too**

young to know right from wrong, will go into the land. I will give it to them. Your children will take the land for their own.

Deuteronomy 2:31
The Lord said to me, "See, I have begun to deliver Shihon and his country over to you. **Now begin to conquer and possess his land."**

Deuteronomy 3:18
I commanded you at that time, **"The Lord your God has given you this land to take possession of it.** But all your able-bodied men, armed for battle, must cross over ahead of the other Israelites."

Deuteronomy 3:20
But you must **help your Israelite relatives until they take the land that the Lord is giving them** on the other side of the Jordan River. Help them until the Lord gives them peace there, just as he did for you here. **Then you may come back to this land that I have given you.**

Deuteronomy 3:28
You must give instructions to Joshua. Encourage him. Make him strong, because Joshua must lead the people across the Jordan River. You can see the land, but **Joshua will lead them into that land. He will help them take the land and live in it.**

Deuteronomy 4:1

Now, Israel, hear the decrees and laws I am about to teach you. Follow them so **that you may live and may go in and take possession of the land the Lord, the God of your ancestors, is giving you.**

Deuteronomy 4:5

See, I have taught you decrees and laws as the Lord my God commanded me, so that you may **follow them in the land you are entering to take possession of it.**

Deuteronomy 4:14

And the Lord directed me at that time to teach you **the decrees and laws you are to follow in the land that you are crossing the Jordan to possess.**

Deuteronomy 4:38

When you moved forward, he forced you out nations that were greater and more powerful than you. **And he led you into their land. He gave you their land to live in, as he is still doing today.**

Deuteronomy 4:40

Keep his decrees and commands, which I am giving you today, so that it may go well with you and your children after you and that you may live long in the land the Lord your God gives you for all time.

Deuteronomy 6:3
Hear, Israel, and be careful to obey so that it may go well with you and that you may increase greatly in a land flowing with milk and honey, just as the Lord, the God of your ancestors, promised you.

Deuteronomy 6:10
The Lord your God made a promise to your ancestors, Abraham, Isaac, and Jacob. He promised to give you this land, and he will give it to you. He will give you great and rich cities that you did not build.

Deuteronomy 6:18
Do what is right and good in the Lord's sight, so that it may go well with you and you may go in and take over the good land the Lord promised on oath to your ancestors.

Deuteronomy 6:23
But he brought us out from there to bring us in and give us the land he promised on oath to our ancestors.

Deuteronomy 7:1
The Lord your God will lead you into the land that you are entering to take for your own. He will force out many nations for you, the Hittites, Girgashites, Amorites, Canaanites, Perizzites, Hivites, and Jebusites, seven nations greater and more powerful than you.

Deuteronomy 7:13
He will love you and bless you and increase your numbers. He will bless the fruit of your womb, the crops of your land, your grain, new wine, olive oil and the calves of your herds and the lambs of your flocks **in the land he swore to your ancestors to give you.**

Deuteronomy 8:1
All the commandment which I command thee this day shall you observe to do, that ye may live, and multiply, and **go in and possess the land which Jehovah swore to your fathers.**

Deuteronomy 8:10
When you have eaten and are satisfied, **praise the Lord your God for the good land he has given you.**

Deuteronomy 9:5
It is not because of your righteousness or your integrity that **you are going in to take possession of their land;** but on

account of the wickedness of these nations, the Lord your God will drive them out before you, **to accomplish what he swore to your fathers, to Abraham, Isaac and Jacob.**

Deuteronomy 9:23
When the Lord sent you out from Kadesh Barnea, he said, "**Go up and take possession of the land I have given you.**" But you rebelled against the command of the Lord your God. You did not trust him or obey him.

Deuteronomy 10:11
"**Go**" the Lord said to me, "and lead the people on their way **so that they may enter and possess the land I swore to their ancestors to give them.**"

Deuteronomy 11:8-9
Observe therefore all the commands I am giving you today, so that you may have the strength to **go in and take over the land that you are crossing the Jordan to possess, and so that you may live long in the land the Lord swore to your ancestors to give to them and their descendants, a land flowing with milk and honey.**

Deuteronomy 11:21
Then both **you and your children will live a long time in the**

land that the Lord promised to give to your ancestors. You
will live there as long as the skies are above the earth.

Deuteronomy 11:31
You are to cross over the Jordan to **go in to take possession
of the land that the Lord your God is giving you.**

Deuteronomy 12:1
These are the decrees and laws you must be careful **to follow
in the land that the Lord, the God of your ancestors, has
given you to possess**, as long as you live in the land.

Deuteronomy 12:10
But you will cross the Jordan and **settle in the land the Lord
your God is giving you as an inheritance,** and he will give you
rest from all your enemies around you so that you will live in
safety.

Deuteronomy 16:20
Follow justice and justice alone, **so that you may live and
possess the land the Lord your God is giving you.**

Deuteronomy 17:14
When you enter the land the Lord your God is giving you and

have taken possession of it and settled in it, and you say, "Let us set a king over us like all the nations around us."

Deuteronomy 18:9
When you **enter the land the Lord your God is giving you**, do not learn to imitate the detestable ways of the nation's there.

Deuteronomy 19:1-3
When the Lord your God has destroyed the nations whose land he is giving you, and when you have driven them out and settled in their towns and houses, then set aside for yourselves three cities **in the land the Lord your God is giving you to possess**. Determine the distances involved and **divide into three parts the land the Lord your God is giving you as an inheritance.**

Deuteronomy 19:14
Do not move your neighbor's boundary stone set up by your predecessors in the inheritance you receive **in the land the Lord your God is giving you to possess.**

Deuteronomy 21:1-2
"**In the land that the Lord your God is giving you,** you might find a dead body in a field, but no one knows who killed that person. Your leaders and judges must come out and measure the distance to the towns around the dead body."

Deuteronomy 21: 22-23

"And if a man has committed a crime punishable by death and you hang him on a tree, his body shall not remain all night on the tree, but you shall bury him the same day, for a hanged man is cursed by God. **You shall not defile your land that the Lord your God is giving you for an inheritance.**"

Deuteronomy 24:1-4

"**And you shall not bring sin upon the land that the Lord your God is giving you for an inheritance.**"

Deuteronomy 25:15

You must have accurate and honest weights and measures, so **that you may live long in the land the Lord your God is giving you.**

Deuteronomy 25:19

When the Lord your God gives you rest from all the enemies around you **in the land he is giving you to possess as an inheritance,** you shall blot out the name of Amalek from under heaven. Do not forget!

Deuteronomy 26:1-3

When you have entered the land the Lord your God is giving you as an inheritance and have taken possession of it and settled in it, take some of the firstfruits of all that you produce from the soil of **the land the Lord your God is giving you** and put them in a basket. Then go to the place the Lord your God will choose as a dwelling for his Name and say to the priest in office at the time, "I declare today to the Lord your God that **I have come to the land the Lord swore to our ancestors to give us.**"

Deuteronomy 26:9-10

He brought **us to this place and gave us this land, a land flowing with milk and honey**; and now I bring the firstfruits of the soil that you, Lord, has given me.

Deuteronomy 26:15

"Look down from heaven, your holy dwelling place, and bless your people Israel and **the land you have given us as you promised on oath to our ancestors, a land flowing with milk and honey.**"

Deuteronomy 27:2-3

When you have crossed the Jordan into the land the Lord your God is giving you, set up some large stones and coat them with plaster. Write on them all the words of this law **when you have crossed over to enter the land the Lord your God is giving you, a land flowing with milk and honey, just as the Lord, the God of your ancestors, promised you.**

Deuteronomy 28:11

The Lord will grant you abundant prosperity in the fruit of your womb, the young of your livestock and the crops of your ground **in the land he swore to your ancestors to give you.**

Deuteronomy 28:52

"They shall besiege you in all your towns, until your high and fortified walls, in which you trusted, come down throughout all your land. And they shall besiege you **in all your towns throughout all your land, which the Lord your God has given you.**"

Deuteronomy 30:3-5

Then the Lord your God will restore your fortune and have compassion on you and gather you again from all the nations where he scattered you. Even if you have been banished to the most distant land under the heavens, from there the Lord your God will gather you and bring you back. **He will bring you to the land that belonged to your ancestors, and you will take possession of it**. He will make you more prosperous and numerous than your ancestors.

Deuteronomy 30:19-20

This day I call the heavens and the earth as witnesses against you that I have set before you life and death, blessings and curses. Now choose life, so that you and your children may live and that you may love the Lord your God, listen to his voice, and hold fast to him. For the Lord is your life, and **he will give you many years in the land he swore to give to your fathers, Abraham, Isaac and Jacob.**

Deuteronomy 31:7
Then Moses summoned Joshua and said to him in the presence of all Israel, "Be strong and courageous, **for you must go with this people into the land that the Lord swore to their ancestors to give them, and you must divide it among them as their inheritance."**

Deuteronomy 31:20
I will take them into the land that I promised to give to their ancestors, a land filled with many good things. And they will have all they want to eat. They will have a rich life.

Deuteronomy 31:21
And when many disasters and calamities come on them, this song will testify against them, because it will not be forgotten by their descendants. I know what they are disposed to do, even **before I bring them into the land I promised them on oath**.

Deuteronomy 31:23
The Lord gave this command to Joshua son of Nun: "Be strong and courageous, **for you will bring the Israelites into the land I promised them on oath, and I myself will be with you.**

Deuteronomy 32:52

"Therefore, you will see the land only from a distance; **you will not enter the land I am giving to the people of Israel.**"

Deuteronomy 34:4

Then the Lord said to him, **"This is the land I promised on oath to Abraham, Isaac and Jacob when I said; I will give it to your descendants.** I have let you see it with your eyes, but you will not cross over into it."

Joshua - Yehoshu'a

Joshua 1:2-4

Moses my servant is dead. Now then, you and all these people, **get ready to cross the Jordan River into the land I am about to give to the Israelites.** I will give you every place where you set your foot, as I promised Moses. **Your territory will extend from the desert to Lebanon, and from the great river, the Euphrates, all the Hittite country to the Mediterranean Sea in the west.**

Joshua 1:6

"Be strong and courageous, because **you will lead these people to inherit the land I swore to their ancestors to give them.**"

Joshua 1:11

Go through the camp and tell the people; "Get your provisions ready. **Three days from now you will cross the Jordan here to go in and take possession of the land the Lord your God is giving you for your own.**"

Joshua 1:15

The Lord has given you a place to live, and he will do the same for your brothers. But you must **help them until they take control of the land the Lord your God is giving them.** Then you can come back and settle here on the east side of the river. **This is the land that the Lord's servant Moses said would be yours.**

Joshua 2:9

And said to them, **"I know that the Lord has given you this land** and that a great fear of you has fallen on us, so that all who live in this country are melting in fear because of you."

Joshua 2:14

"Our lives for your lives!" the men assured her. "If you don't tell what we are doing, **we will treat you kindly and faithfully when the Lord gives us the land."**

Joshua 2:24

They said to Joshua, **"The Lord has surely given the whole land into our hands;** all the people are melting in fear because of us."

Joshua 11:23

So Joshua took the entire land, just as the Lord had directed

Moses, and he gave it as an inheritance to Israel according to their tribal divisions. Then the land had rest from war.

Joshua 13:1

When Joshua had grown old, the Lord said to him, **"You are now very old, and there are still very large areas of land to be taken over."**

Joshua 14:9

So on that day Moses swore to me, **"The land on which your feet have walked will be your inheritance and that of your children forever,** because you have followed the Lord my God wholeheartedly."

Joshua 18:1-3

Then the whole congregation of the people of Israel assembled at Shiloh and set up the tent of meeting there. The land lay subdued before them. There remained among the people of Israel seven tribes whose inheritance had not yet been apportioned. So Joshua said to the people of Israel, **"How long will you put off going into take possession of the land, which the Lord, the God of your fathers, has given you?**

Joshua 18:10

Joshua then cast lots for them in Shiloh in the presence of the

Lord, and<u>t here he distributed the land to the Israelites</u>
<u>according to their tribal divisions.</u>

Joshua 19:51

<u>These are the territories</u> that Eleazar the priest, Joshua son of
Nun and the heads of the tribal clans of Israel **assigned by lot**
at Shiloh in the presence of the Lord at the entrance to the
tent of meeting. **And so they finished dividing the land.**

Joshua 21:43

The Lord gave Israel all the land he had sworn to give their
ancestors, and they took possession of it and settled there.

Joshua 23:5

The Lord your God will force the people living there to leave.
You will take that land. The Lord will force them to leave,
just as he promised.

Joshua 24:8

<u>I brought you to the land of the Amorites</u> who lived east of the
Jordan. They fought against you, but I gave them into your
hands. I will drive them out before you, and **you will take**
possession of their land, as the Lord your God promised you.

Joshua 24: 13

<u>So I gave you a land on which you did not toil and cities you did not build;</u> and you live in them and eat from vineyards and olive groves that you did not plant.

Judges - Sof'tim

Judges 2:1-2

The Lord's messenger came up from Gilgal to Bochim and said, "**I brought you up from Egypt and led you into the land that I had promised to your ancestors. I said, I will never break my covenant with you,** and you shall make no covenant with the inhabitants of this land; you shall break down their altars."

1 Kings – M'lakhim Alef

1 Kings 8:33-34

"When your people Israel have been defeated by an enemy because they have sinned against you, and when they turn back to you and give praise to your name, praying and making supplication to you in this temple, then hear from heaven and forgive the sin of your people Israel and **bring them back to the land you gave to their ancestors.**"

1 Kings 8: 36

Teach them the right way to live, and **send rain on the land you gave your people for an inheritance.**

1 Kings 8:37- 40

"If there is a famine in the land caused by plant disease or locusts or caterpillars, or if Israel's enemies besiege one of her cities, or if the people are struck by an epidemic or plague—or whatever the problem is—then when the people realize their sin and pray toward this Temple hear them from heaven and forgive and answer all who have made an honest confession; for you know each heart. In this way they will always learn to reverence you **as they continue to live in this land that you have given their fathers.**"

2 Kings - M'lakhim Bet

2 Kings 21:8

"I will not again make the feet of the Israelites **wander from the land I gave their ancestors,** if only they will be careful to do everything I commanded them and will keep the whole Law that my servant Moses gave them."

1 Chronicles – Divrei–Ha Yamim Alef

1 Chronicles 16:13-18

O offspring of Israel his servant, children of Jacob, his chosen ones, He is the Lord our God; his judgments are in all the earth. <u>He remembers his covenant forever, the promise he made, for a thousand generations, the covenant he made with Abraham, the oath he swore to Isaac. He confirmed it to Jacob as a decree, to Israel as an everlasting covenant: "To you I will give the land of Canaan as the portion you will inherit."</u>

2 Chronicles – Divrei–Ha Yamim Bet

2 Chronicles 6:24-25
"If your people Israel are defeated before the enemy because they have sinned against you, and they turn again and acknowledge your name and pray and plead with you in this house, then hear from heaven and forgive the sin of your people Israel **and bring them again to the land that you gave to them and to their fathers."**

2 Chronicles 6:26-27
"When heaven is shut up and there is no rain because they have sinned against you, if they pray toward this place and acknowledge your name and turn from their sin, when you afflict them, then hear in heaven and forgive the sin of your servants, your people Israel, when you teach them the good way in which they should walk, and **grant rain upon your land, which you have given to your people as an inheritance."**

2 Chronicles 6:38-39
And if they turn back to you with all their heart and soul in the land of their captivity where they were taken, and **pray toward the land you gave their ancestors,** toward the city you have

chosen and toward the temple I have built for your Name, then hear from the heavens, even from thy dwelling place, their prayer and their supplications, and maintain their cause, and forgive thy forgive thy people which have sinned against thee.

2 Chronicles 33:8
I will not again make the feet of the Israelites leave **the land I assigned to your ancestors,** if only they will be careful to do everything I commanded them concerning all the laws, decrees and regulations given through Moses."

Nehemiah – Nechemyah

Nehemiah 9:7-8

"You are the Lord God, who chose Abram and brought him out of Ur of the Chaldeans and named him Abraham. You found his heart faithful to you, and **you made a covenant with him to give to his descendants the land of the Canaanites, Hittites, Amorites, Perizzites, Jebusites and Girgashites.** You have kept your promise because you are righteous."

Nehemiah 9:15

In their hunger you gave them bread from heaven and in their thirst you brought them water from the rock; **you told them to go in and take possession of the land you had sworn with uplifted hand to give them.**

Nehemiah 9:36

"But see, we are slaves today, **slaves in the land you gave our ancestors** so they could eat its fruit and the other good things it produces."

Psalms – Tehillim

Psalms 105:8-11
He remembers his covenant forever, the promise he made, for a thousand generations; the covenant he made with Abraham the oath he swore to Isaac. He confirmed it to Jacob as a decree, to Israel as an everlasting covenant; "To you I will give the land of Canaan as the portion you will inherit."

Psalms 105:42-44
He remembered his holy promise given to his servant Abraham. He brought out his people with rejoicing, his chosen ones with shouts of joy; he gave them the lands of the nations, and they took possession to what others had toiled for.

Psalms 135:12
He gave their land as an inheritance, an inheritance to his people Israel.

Psalms 136:21-22
He gave their land as an inheritance. His love endures forever.

Isaiah – Yesha'yahu

Isaiah 14:1-2

<u>**When the Lord will have compassion on Jacob and again**</u> <u>**choose Israel, and settle them in their own land**</u>, then strangers will join them and attach themselves to the house of Jacob. The peoples will take them along and bring them to their place, and **the house of Israel will possess them as an** **inheritance in the land of the Lord** as male servants and female servants; and they will take their captors captive and will rule over their oppressors.

Isaiah 49:8

Thus say's the Lord, "In the time of my favor I will answer you, and in the day of salvation I will help you; **I will keep you and** **will make you to be a covenant for the people to restore the** **land and to reassign its desolate inheritances."**

Isaiah 61:7

Instead of your shame you will receive a double portion and instead of disgrace you will rejoice in your inheritance. And so **you will inherit a double portion in your land**, and everlasting joy will be yours.

Jeremiah – Yirmeyahu

Jeremiah 3:16-19

It shall be in those days, when your numbers have increased greatly in the land," declares the Lord, "people will no longer say, 'The ark of the covenant of the Lord.' It will never enter their minds or be remembered; it will not be missed, nor will another one be made. At that time they will call Jerusalem, The Throne of the Lord and all nations will gather in Jerusalem to honor the name of the Lord. No longer will they follow the stubbornness of their evil hearts. In those days the people of Judah will join the people of Israel, and together **they will come from a northern land to the land I gave your ancestors as an inheritance.** I myself said, **"How gladly would I treat you like my children and give you a pleasant land, the most beautiful inheritance of any nation,** I thought you would call me 'Father' and not turn away from following me."

Jeremiah 11:5

"Then I will fulfill the oath I swore to your ancestors, to give them a land flowing with milk and honey, the land you possess today."

Jeremiah 16:14-15

But there will come a glorious day, says the Lord, when the whole topic of conversation will be that God is bringing his people home from a nation in the north, and from many other lands where he had scattered them. You will look back no longer to the time when I can rescue you from your slavery in Egypt. That mighty miracle will scarcely be mentioned anymore. **Yes, I will bring you back again, says the Lord, to this same land I gave your fathers.**

Jeremiah 23:7-8

"So then, the days are coming," declares the Lord, when people will no longer say, "As surely as the Lord lives, who brought the Israelites up out of Egypt," but they will say, "As surely as the Lord lives, who brought the descendants of Israel up out of the land of the north and out of all the countries where he had banished them. **Then they will live in their own land.**"

Jeremiah 24:6

My eyes will watch over them for their good, and **I will bring them back to this land.** I will build them up and not tear them down; I will plant them and not uproot them.

Jeremiah 25:5

They said, "Turn now, each of you, from your evil ways and your evil practices, and **you can stay in the land the Lord gave to you and your ancestors for ever and ever.**"

Jeremiah 30:3

The days are coming,' declares the Lord, 'when **I will bring my people Israel and Judah back from captivity and restore them to the land I gave their ancestors to possess,**' says the Lord."

Jeremiah 32:22

You gave them this land you had sworn to give their ancestors, a land flowing with milk and honey.

Jeremiah 32:41

I will rejoice in doing them good and will **assuredly plant them in this land with all my heart and soul.**

Ezekiel – Yechezkel

Ezekiel 20:40-42

"For on my holy mountain, the high mountain of Israel,"
declares the Sovereign Lord, "there in the land all the people
of Israel will serve me, and there I will accept them. There I
will require your offerings and your choice gifts, along with all
your holy sacrifices. I will accept you as fragrant incense when I
bring you out from the nations and gather you from the
countries where you have been scattered, and I will be proved
holy through you in the sight of the nations. Then you will
know that I am the Lord, **when I bring you into the land of
Israel, the land I had sworn with uplifted hand to give to your
ancestors.**"

Ezekiel 28:25

This is what the Sovereign Lord says: "When I gather the
people of Israel from the nations where they have been
scattered, I will be proved holy through them in the sight of
the nations. **Then they will live in their own land, which I
gave to my servant Jacob.**"

Ezekiel 34:13

I will bring them out from the nations and gather them from

the countries, and **I will bring them into their own land.** I will pasture them on the mountains of Israel, in the ravines and in all the settlements in the land.

Ezekiel 36:24
"For I will take you out of the nations; **I will gather you from all the countries and bring you back into your own land."**

Ezekiel 36:28
Then you will live in the land I gave your ancestors; you will be my people, and I will be your God.

Ezekiel 37:11-14
"Son of man, these bones are the people of Israel;" They say, "Our bones are dried up and our hope is gone; we are cut off." Therefore prophesy and say to them: This is what the Sovereign Lord says: "My people, I am going to open your graves and bring you up from them; **I will bring you back to the land of Israel.** Then you, my people, will know that I am the Lord, when I open your graves and bring you up from them. I will put my Spirit in you and you will live, and **I will settle you in your own land.** Then you will know that I the Lord have spoken, and I have done it, declares the Lord."

Ezekiel 37:21-22
"This is what the Sovereign Lord says; I will take the Israelites out of the nations where they have gone. **I will gather them**

from all around and bring them back into their own land. I will
make them one nation in the land, on the mountains of Israel.
There will be one king over all of them and they will never again
be two nations or be divided into two kingdoms."

Ezekiel 37:25
They will live in the land I gave to my servant Jacob, the
land where your ancestors lived. They and their children and
their children's children will live there forever, and David my
servant will be their prince forever

Ezekiel 39:28
Then they will know that I am the Lord their God, for though I
sent them into exile among the nations, I will gather them to
their own land, not leaving any behind.

Ezekiel 47:13-14
The Sovereign Lord says: "These are the boundaries of the land
that you will divide among the twelve tribes of Israel as their
inheritance, with two portions for Joseph. You are to divide it
equally among them. Because I swore with uplifted hand to give
it to your ancestors, this land will become your inheritance."

Ezekiel 47:21
"You are to distribute this land among yourselves according to
the tribes of Israel."

Ezekiel 48:29

"<u>This is the land you are to allot as an inheritance to the Tribes of Israel,</u> and these will be their portions," declares the Sovereign Lord.

Amos – Amos

Amos 9:14
<u>I will bring my people, Israel, back from captivity. They will rebuild the ruined cities, and they will live in them.</u> They will plant vineyards and drink the wine they produce. They will plant gardens and eat the crops they produce.

Amos 9:15
<u>"I will plant Israel in their own land never again to be uprooted from the land I have given them,"</u> says the Lord your God.

Micah – Mikhah

Micah 4:8

O tower of the flock, hill of the daughter of Zion, <u>**your former**</u> <u>**sovereignty will return, the royal power of the daughter of**</u> <u>**Jerusalem.**</u>

Contact Us If You Are Interested In:

- Participating in Kehilat HaMishkan Ministry in Hawaii
- Participating in the 'The Hawaii-Israel Alignment'
- Participating in 'The America-Israel Alignment' – Align your State with Israel
- Participating in a Gideon's Army of 300 Shofar Blowers to Jerusalem
- Planting an Olive Tree in Israel from your Hawaii District
- Financially Supporting the Hawaii-Israel Alignment (HIA)
- The Hawaii House Embassy in Jerusalem
- The Israeli House Embassy in Hawaii

The Hawaii-Israel Alignment

(Oahu) 808-330-8893   (Maui) 808-357-3303

nowlincorrea@yahoo.com shalommaui@aol.com

Oahu 808-330-8893   Maui 808-357-3303

www.ingramcontent.com/pod-product-compliance
Lightning Source LLC
Chambersburg PA
CBHW060041040426
42331CB00032B/1998